Read to Me, Mommy

This edition is published by JellyBean Press,
distributed by
Random House Value Publishing, Inc.
40 Engelhard Avenue
Avenel, New Jersey 07001

Random House
New York • Toronto • London • Sydney • Auckland

Cover painting by Gary Overacre

Printed and bound in the United States of America

Library of Congress Cataloging-in-Publication Data
Read to me, mommy.
p. cm.
Summary: A collection including poems and such traditional stories as
"The Three Billy Goats Gruff," "Johnny and the Three Goats," and
"The Bremen Town Musicians." 1. Tales. [1. Children's poetry. 2. Folklore.
3. Poetry—Collections.]
PZ5.R198445 1995
808.8'99282—dc20
94-39815
CIP
AC

ISBN 0-517-12326-6

8 7 6 5 4 3 2 1

Read to Me, Mommy

Edited by Glorya Hale
Designed by Liz Trovato

JellyBean Press
New York • Avenel

CONTENTS

INTRODUCTION

"Read to me, Mommy" is a familiar plea at bedtime, on a rainy afternoon, or whenever a child just wants to sit close to you and share a trip to the land of Let's Pretend or listen quietly as you recite poems that you may remember from your own childhood.

No one knows who first told the stories that are retold in this book. We know they are very old and we can imagine how many of them came into existence. Perhaps, one cold winter evening many hundreds of years ago, a woman's children gathered around her and one of them said, "Please tell us a story." Of course, the mother knew many stories and told them over and over again. And her children never tired of listening to them and entering the marvelous place where animals could speak and were frequently smarter than humans.

Those children grew up and told the same stories to their own children, who told them to their children. And so the tales were handed down from generation to generation until

they were written down and published in books so all mothers could read them to their children.

From this book you can read the story of the three billy goats Gruff, who outwit a mean, hungry troll, and the tale of the Bremen Town Musicians—four old animals who find a fine home to share. No one can help but sympathize with Johnny, the farmer's son, who tries to get his goats out of Mr. Smith's turnip field, or laugh at the antics of the fox who travels from farm to farm carrying a big bag.

Also included here are Elizabeth Gordon's amusing verses about *Flower Children* and a delightful selection of poems, many chosen from *A Child's Garden of Verses* by Robert Louis Stevenson.

This lovely book, wonderfully illustrated by such well-known artists as Frederick Richardson, Anne Anderson, and Margaret W. Tarrant, will surely bring back memories of your own delight when you were read to. And now you can share with your child many marvelous journeys to the faraway land of Let's Pretend that was discovered long, long ago by other mothers.

GLORYA HALE

The Three Billy Goats Gruff

nce upon a time there were three billy goats. They were brothers and their names were Tiny Billy Goat Gruff, Big Billy Goat Gruff, and Great Big Billy Goat Gruff. Their family had always lived in a meadow on a hillside where there was lots of green grass and many delicious little plants for them to eat. But one summer it did not rain for many weeks. The grass got brown and tasted terrible. And the three billy goats had eaten all the sweet little plants. As the days passed they got hungrier and hungrier and thinner and thinner.

Farther up the hillside there was a big meadow covered with fresh green grass. The billy goat brothers knew that in this other meadow they could eat and eat and eat until they were plump once again. But there was a problem: to get to that meadow they would have to cross a bridge over a stream, and the bridge belonged to an ugly troll who lived beneath it. The troll had eyes as big as saucers, a nose as long as your arm, and a bushy green beard. His favorite food was billy goat.

Finally, the three billy goats became so hungry that they decided they had to go to the big meadow. They set off early in the morning and by noon they reached the bridge. Tiny Billy Goat Gruff was the first to cross.

"Trip, trap; trip, trap!" His tiny hooves made a little tapping sound as he walked over the wooden bridge.

"Who is that trip-trapping over my bridge?" roared the troll in a booming voice that made the bridge shake.

"Oh! It is only I, Tiny Billy Goat Gruff. I'm going up to the big meadow on the hillside where I can eat and eat until I'm plump again," said the little billy goat in a small, quavering voice.

"Well, I think I'm the one who is going to eat," bellowed the troll. "I'm going to eat you!"

"Oh, no! Please don't eat me, sir. I'm too little, I am, I am," said Tiny Billy Goat Gruff. "I would hardly make a mouthful for you. Wait a little while until my brother Big Billy Goat Gruff comes along. He's much bigger than I am."

"Well, all right," said the troll. "Be off with you now."

It was not long until Big Billy Goat Gruff began to cross the bridge.

"TRIP, TRAP! TRIP, TRAP! TRIP, TRAP!" His big hooves made a big tapping sound as he walked over the wooden bridge.

"Who is that trip-trapping over my bridge?" roared the troll in his thundering voice.

"Oh! It is I, Big Billy Goat Gruff. I'm going up to the big meadow on the hillside to eat and eat until I'm plump again," said the big billy goat, who had quite a loud voice.

"I'm the one who is going to have a good meal," boomed the troll. "I'm going to eat you!"

"Oh, you don't want to eat me," said Big Billy Goat Gruff. "I'm just skin and bones. There's no flesh on me. I won't make a decent meal for you. Wait until my brother Great Big Billy Goat Gruff comes along. He's much bigger than I am."

"Very well!" said the troll. "Be off with you."

Just then Great Big Billy Goat Gruff began to cross the bridge.

"TRIP, TRAP! TRIP, TRAP! TRIP, TRAP!" His great big hooves made a great big sound. This billy goat was so heavy that the bridge creaked and groaned under him.

"Who is that trip-trapping over my bridge?" thundered the troll.

"It's I! Great Big Billy Goat Gruff," the billy goat replied in a very deep and very loud voice.

"Well, I hope you are not planning to go up to the big meadow with your brothers," roared the troll, climbing onto the bridge, "because you are going to be my lunch."

"That's what you think," roared back the great big billy goat as he lowered his head and butted the troll, tossing him out into the deepest part of the stream. Then, knowing that the troll would never return to his home under the

bridge, Great Big Billy Goat Gruff continued walking to the big meadow on the hillside. There the grass was high and fresh and green. There were more delicious little plants than he had ever seen before.

The three billy goat brothers ate and ate and ate until they got so plump they were scarcely able to walk home again.

Summer Sun

Great is the sun, and wide he goes
Through empty heaven without repose;
And in the blue and glowing days
More thick than rain he showers his rays.

Though closer still the blinds we pull
To keep the shady parlor cool,

Yet he will find a chink or two
To slip his golden fingers through.

The dusty attic spider-clad
He, through the keyhole, maketh glad,
And through the broken edge of tiles,
Into the laddered hayloft smiles.

Meantime his golden face around
He bares to all the garden ground,
And sheds a warm and glittering look
Among the ivy's inmost nook.

Above the hills, along the blue,
Round the bright air with footing true,
To please the child, to paint the rose,
The gardener of the world, he goes.

ROBERT LOUIS STEVENSON

The Wind

Who has seen the wind?
  Neither I nor you:
But when the leaves hang trembling
  The wind is passing through.

Who has seen the wind?
  Neither you nor I:
But when the trees bow down their heads
  The wind is passing by.

CHRISTINA ROSSETTI

Mr. Nobody

I know a funny little man,
  As quiet as a mouse,
Who does the mischief that is done
  In everybody's house!
There's no one ever sees his face,
  And yet we all agree
That every plate we break was cracked
  By Mr. Nobody.

'Tis he who always tears our books,
  Who leaves the door ajar,
He pulls the buttons from our shirts,
  And scatters pins afar;
The papers always are mislaid,
  Who had them last but he?
There's no one tosses them about
  But Mr. Nobody.

The fingermarks upon the door
  By none of us are made;
We never leave the blinds unclosed,
  To let the curtains fade.
The ink we never spill; the boots
  That lying round you see
Are not our boots;—they all belong
  To Mr. Nobody.

AUTHOR UNKNOWN

The COCK, The MOUSE, and the LITTLE RED HEN

Once upon a time there was a pretty little house. It had a little green door and four little windows with green shutters. The house was on a hill and in the house lived a cock, a mouse, and a little red hen.

Not too far away, there was another little house. It was not pretty. It had a door that wouldn't shut, two of the windows were broken, and all the paint had peeled off the shutters. In this house lived a big bad fox and his four bad little foxes.

One morning the four little foxes went to the big fox and said, "Oh, Father, we're so hungry!"

"We had nothing to eat yesterday," said one.

"And scarcely anything the day before," said another.

"We shared a half a chicken the day before that," said the third.

"And we only had two little ducks to share the day before that," said the fourth.

The big fox shook his head for a time, for he was thinking. At last he said in a big gruff voice, "On the hill over there is a house. And in that house lives a cock."

"And a mouse," screamed two of the little foxes.

"And a little red hen," screamed the other two.

"And they are nice and plump," continued the big fox. "This very day, I'll take my great sack and I will go up that hill, and into that house, and into my sack I will put the cock, the mouse, and the little red hen."

"I'll make a fire to roast the cock," said one little fox.

"I'll put on the saucepan filled with water to boil the hen," said the second.

"And I'll get the frying pan to fry the mouse," said the third.

"And I'll have the biggest helping when they are cooked," said the fourth little fox, who was the greediest of them all.

The four little foxes jumped for joy as the big fox went to get his sack and prepared to start on his journey.

But what was happening to the cock and the mouse and the little red hen, all this time?

Well, sad to say, the cock and the mouse had both gotten out of bed on the wrong side that morning. The cock complained that the day was too hot. The mouse grumbled because it was too cold.

Grumbling and complaining they came down to the kitchen where the good little red hen, looking as bright as a sunbeam, was bustling about.

"Who'll get some twigs to start the fire with?" she asked.

"I won't," said the cock.

"I won't," said the mouse.

"Then I'll do it myself," said the little red hen. And off she ran to get the twigs.

"And now, who will fill the kettle from the spring?" she asked when she returned.

"I won't," said the cock.

"I won't," said the mouse.

"Then I'll do it myself," said the little red hen. And off she ran to fill the kettle with water from the spring

"And who will get the breakfast ready?" she asked as she put the kettle on the fire to boil the water.

"I won't," said the cock.

"I won't," said the mouse.

"Well, I'll do it myself," said the little red hen.

All during breakfast the cock and the mouse quarreled and grumbled. The cock upset the milk jug and the mouse scattered crumbs on the floor.

"Who'll clear away the breakfast things?" asked the poor little red hen, hoping they would soon stop being so cranky and cross.

"I won't," said the cock.

"I won't," said the mouse.

"Then I'll do it myself," said the little red hen.

So she cleared everything away, swept up the crumbs, and brushed the ashes from the hearth.

"And now, who will help me to make the beds?"

"I won't," said the cock.

"I won't," said the mouse.

"Then I'll do it myself," said the little red hen. And she tripped away upstairs.

The lazy cock and the grumbling mouse sat down in comfortable armchairs near the fire. Both of them soon fell fast asleep.

Now the big bad fox had crept up the hill and into the garden. If the cock and the mouse hadn't been asleep, they would surely have seen his sharp eyes peeping in at the window. "Rat tat tat. Rat tat tat," the fox knocked at the door.

"Who can that be?" asked the mouse, half opening his eyes.

"Go and look for yourself, if you want to know," said the rude cock.

Perhaps it's the postman, thought the mouse, and he may have a letter for me. So without waiting to ask who it was, he lifted the latch and opened the door.

As soon as he opened it, in jumped the big fox. He had a cruel smile upon his face!

"Oh! Oh! Oh!" squeaked the mouse as he tried to run up the chimney.

"Doodle doodle do!" screamed the cock as he jumped on the back of the biggest armchair.

But the fox only laughed, and in a flash he grabbed the little mouse by the tail and popped him into the sack. Then he seized the cock by the neck and popped him in, too.

Then the little red hen came running downstairs to see what all the noise was about. And the fox caught her and put her into the sack with the mouse

and the cock. Then he took a long piece of string, wound it round and round and round the mouth of the sack, and tied it very tight. He then threw the sack over his back, and off he went down the hill.

"Oh! I wish I hadn't been so cross," said the cock as they bumped about inside the sack.

"Oh! I wish I hadn't been so lazy," said the mouse, wiping the tears from his eyes with the tip of his tail.

"It's never too late to change," said the little red hen. "Don't be too sad. See, here I have my little workbag, and in it there is a pair of scissors, a little thimble, a needle, and some thread. Very soon you will see what I am going to do."

The sun was very hot and the sack was quite heavy. Soon Mr. Fox began to feel tired. He thought it might be a good idea to lie down under a tree and go to sleep for a little while. So he threw the sack down with a big bump and stretched out in the shade of a big tree. He fell fast asleep and began to snore.

As soon as the little red hen heard the fox snoring, she took out her scissors and began to snip a hole in the sack that was just large enough for the mouse to creep through.

"Quick," she whispered to the mouse, "run as fast as you can and bring back a stone about the same size as you are."

Out scampered the mouse. He soon came back, pushing a stone before him.

"Push it in here," said the little red hen, and in a twinkling he pushed the stone into the sack.

Then the little red hen snipped away at the hole. Soon it was large enough for the cock to get through.

"Quick," she said, "run and get a stone as big as you are."

Out flew the cock, and he soon came back quite out of breath with a large stone, which he pushed into the sack.

Then the little red hen popped out, got a stone as big as herself, and pushed it in. Next she put on her thimble, took out her needle and thread, and sewed

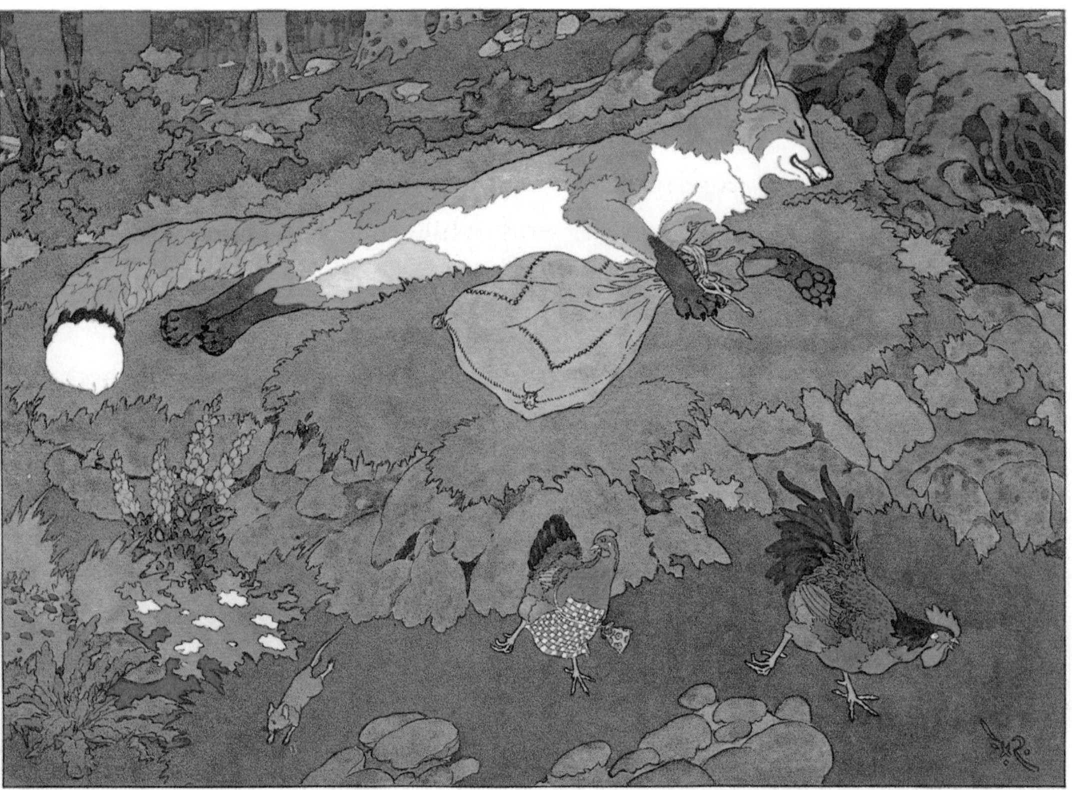

up the hole as quickly as ever she could. When she was finished, the cock and the mouse and the little red hen ran home as fast as they could go. They shut the door behind them, drew the bolts, closed the shutters, and pulled down the blinds. Now they felt quite safe inside their pretty little house.

The fox lay fast asleep under the tree for some time, but finally he woke up.

"Dear, dear," he said, rubbing his eyes and then looking at the long shadows on the grass, "how late it is getting. I must hurry home."

So the big fox went grumbling and groaning down the hill, until he came to the stream.

Splash! In went one foot. Splash! In went the other, but the stones in the sack were so heavy that at the very next step down tumbled Mr. Fox into a deep pool.

And then the fishes must have carried him off to their fairy caves and kept him a prisoner there, because he was never seen again. And the four greedy little foxes had to go to bed without any supper.

The cock and the mouse never grumbled again. They lit the fire, filled the kettle, set the table, and did all the work while the good little red hen had a holiday and sat resting in the big armchair. No foxes ever bothered them again, and they are probably still living happily in the little house with the green door and green shutters, which stands on the hill.

Four Paws

Four Paws, the kitten from the farm,
  Is come to live with Betsey Jane,
Leaving the stock-yard for the warm
  Flower-compassed cottage in the lane,
To wash his idle face and play
Among chintz cushions all the day.

Under the shadow of her hair
  He lies, who loves him nor desists
To praise his whiskers and compare
  The tabby bracelets on his wrists,
Omelet at lunch and milk at tea
Suit Betsey Jane and so fares he.

Happy beneath her golden hand
  He purrs contentedly nor hears
His mother mourning through the land,
  The old gray cat with tattered ears
And humble tail and heavy paw
Who brought him up among the straw.

Never by day she ventures nigh,
  But when the dusk grows dim and deep
And moths flit out of the strange sky

And Betsey has been long asleep—
Out of the dark she comes and brings
Her dark maternal offerings,

Some field mouse or a throstle caught
Near netted fruit or in the corn,
Or rat, for this her darling sought
In the old barn where he was born;
And all lest on his dainty bed
Four Paws were faint or underfed.

Only between the twilight hours
Under the windowpanes she walks
Shrewdly among the scented flowers
Nor snaps the soft nasturtium stalks,
Uttering still her plaintive cries
And Four Paws, from the house, replies,

Leaps from his cushion to the floor,
Down the brick passage scantly lit,
Waits wailing at the outer door
Till one arise and open it—
Then from the swinging lantern's light
Runs to his mother in the night.

HELEN PARRY EDEN

The Owl

When it's very, very dark,
  And the fields are very still,
When the lovely singing lark
  Sings no more above the hill;

When the flowers their petals close,
  And the world is all asleep,
Then a hunter hunting goes,
  All among the shadows deep.

Hooting through the woods, he flies
  On his wide and silent wings,
Blinking with his solemn eyes,
  Thinking solemn kinds of things

When the flowers their petals close,
  And the world is all asleep,
Then a hunter hunting goes,
  All among the shadows deep.

GRACE M. TUFFLEY

FLOWER CHILDREN

Lady Tulip, stately dame,
From across the ocean came;
Liked this country very much,
Although she only spoke in Dutch.

Pussy Willow said, "Meow!
Wish someone would tell me how
Other kittens get around
And roll and frolic on the ground."

Pansies like the shaded places,
With their little friendly faces,
Always seem to smile and say,
"How are all the folks today?"

Modest little Violet
Was her loving mother's pet;
Didn't care to go and play,
Rather stay at home all day.

Apple Blossom is a fairy,
Swinging in a tree so airy;
By and by the little sprite
Sprinkles the ground with pink and white.

Little golden-hearted Daisy
Told the sun that she felt lazy;
Said the earth was quite too wet,
She thought she wouldn't open yet.

Geranium wears a scarlet gown,
With trimmings shading into brown,
Her cousin is a dainty sprite,
She dresses modestly in white.

Iris in a country garden,
Politely said, "I beg your pardon,
But I'm from sunny France, you see,
And my real name is Fleur-de-Lis."

Peony's a charming lady,
She doesn't like a spot too shady;
Likes to live out in the light,
Dressed in red or pink or white.

Crimson Rambler one day said,
He didn't like the old homestead;
Thought he'd travel, so he went
Over the wall on mischief bent.

Now let the banners be unfurled,
To greet the fairest of the world;
Come roses all, and pay your duty:
Madame the Queen, American Beauty!

Chrysanthemum is Japanese,
She's a fine lady, if you please;
She comes to see us once a year,
About the time Thanksgiving's here.

In a sweet velvet dress of red,
On Christmas Eve, Poinsettia said
"I'll hang my stocking up because
This is the night for Santa Claus."

Ever see a plant so jolly,
And good fellow-ish as Holly?
Makes no difference what's
    the weather,
He and Christmas come together.

ELIZABETH GORDON

The Upside Down World

I know a place that holds the sky,
A place where little white clouds lie;

The edge is all as green as grass,
The middle is as smooth as glass;

And there the round sun makes his bed;
And there a tree stands on its head;

Sometimes a bird sits on that tree;
Sometimes it sings a song to me;

And always in that shining place
I see a little smiling face;
She nods and smiles; but all the same
The girl down there won't tell her name!

HAMISH HENDRY

THE CAT and THE MOUSE

The cat and the mouse
Played in the malt-house:
The cat bit off the mouse's tail.

"Please, Puss, give me my tail," said the mouse.

"No," said the cat, "I'll not give you your tail until you go to the cow and fetch me some milk."

First she leaped, and then she ran,
Until the mouse came to the cow, and thus began:

"Please, Ms. Cow, give me some milk, so I may give it to the cat, so the cat will give me my tail."

"No," said the cow, "I will give you no milk until you go to the farmer and get me some hay."

First she leaped, and then she ran,
Until the mouse came to the farmer, and thus began:

"Please, Mr. Farmer, give me some hay, so I may give it to the cow, so the cow will give me some milk, so I may give it to the cat, so the cat will give me my own tail."

"No," said the farmer, "I'll give you no hay until you go to the butcher and fetch me some meat."

First she leaped, and then she ran,
Until the mouse came to the butcher, and thus began:

"Please, Mr. Butcher, give me some meat, so I may give it to the farmer, so the farmer will give me some hay, that I may give to the cow, so the cow will give me some milk, so I may give it to the cat, so the cat will give me my own tail."

"No," said the butcher, "I'll give you no meat until you go to the baker and fetch me some bread."

First she leaped, and then she ran,
Until the mouse came to the baker, and thus began:

"Please, Mr. Baker, give me some bread, that I may give to the butcher, so the butcher will give me some meat, that I may give to the farmer, so the farmer will give me some hay, that I may give to the cow, so the cow will give me some milk, that I may give to the cat, so the cat will give me my own tail."

"Yes," said the baker, "I'll give you some bread,
But if you ever eat my flour, I'll cut off your head."

Then the baker gave the mouse some bread, which the mouse gave to the butcher, and the butcher gave the mouse some meat, which the mouse gave to the farmer, and the farmer gave the mouse some hay, which the mouse gave to the cow, and the cow gave the mouse some milk, which the mouse gave to the cat, and the cat gave the mouse her own tail.

Lambkins

On the grassy banks
Lambkins at their pranks;
Woolly sisters, woolly brothers,
  Jumping off their feet,
While their woolly mothers
  Watch by them and bleat.

CHRISTINA ROSSETTI

Busy Bees

The busy bees, they work all day,
And all their work is just like play.
Among the blossoms bright and sunny,
They dance, and hum, and gather honey.

And mother dear, on days like these,
Calls us her little busy bees—
We gather fruit, we sing so gay,
And all our work is just like play!

ANNE ANDERSON

Bubbles

Blowing bubbles! See how fine!
Look at mine! Oh, look at mine!
How they dance, and how they shine—
Mine! Mine! Look at mine!
Mine's like water! Mine's just fine!
Yours is not as big as mine!

ELEANOR FARJEON

Dandelion Messengers

A little bit of dandelion fluff,
If you blow it hard enough,
Will take a message very far!
Perhaps to reach the nearest star.

Anne Anderson

JOHNNY and the THREE GOATS

Every morning in the summer Johnny, the farmer's son, drove his three goats to pasture and every evening when the sun was setting he brought them home again.

One morning Johnny set off bright and early, driving the goats before him and whistling as he trudged along.

Just as he reached Mr. Smith's turnip field he saw there was a broken board in the fence.

The goats saw the broken board, too. Into the field they skipped and began running around and around, stopping now and then to nip off the tops of some tender young turnips.

Johnny knew that he must get the goats out of Mr. Smith's field as quickly as he could. He climbed through the fence and using his big stick he tried to drive the goats back toward their own pasture. But never were there such naughty goats. Around and around they went, not once even looking toward the hole in the fence.

Johnny ran and ran and ran until he could run no more. Then he climbed back through the hole in the fence, sat down at the side of the road, and began to cry.

Just then who should come down the road but the fox. "Good morning, Johnny!" he said. "What are you crying about?"

"I'm crying because I can't get the goats out of the turnip field," said Johnny.

"Oh, don't cry about that," said the fox. "I'll drive them out for you." So over

the fence the fox leaped, and around and around the turnip field he ran after the goats. But they would not even look toward the hole in the fence.

They flicked their tails and shook their heads and away they went, trampling the turnips until it was hard to know what had been growing in the field.

The fox ran until he could run no more. Then he jumped over the fence and sat down beside Johnny. And he began to cry.

Just then down the road came a rabbit. "Good morning, Fox," he said. "What are you crying about?"

"I'm crying because Johnny is crying," said the fox, "and Johnny is crying because he can't get the goats out of the turnip field."

"Tut, tut!" said the rabbit. "What a thing to cry about! Watch me. I'll soon drive them out."

The rabbit hopped through the hole in the fence. Around and around the field he chased the goats, but they would not go anywhere near the hole in the fence. At last the rabbit was so tired he could not hop another hop. He crawled through the hole in the fence, sat down next to the fox, and began to cry.

Just then a bumblebee came buzzing along over the tops of the flowers. When she saw the rabbit she said, "Good morning, Bunny, what are you crying about?"

"I'm crying because the fox is crying," said the rabbit. "And the fox is crying because Johnny is crying, and Johnny is crying because he can't get the goats out of the turnip field."

"Don't cry about that," said the bumblebee. "I'll soon get them out for you."

"You!" said the rabbit. "How could a little thing like you drive the goats out when neither Johnny, nor the fox, nor I can get them out?" And he laughed at the very idea.

"Watch me," said the bumblebee.

Over the fence she flew and buzz-z-z she went right into the ear of the biggest goat.

The goat shook his head and tried to brush away the bumblebee, but the bee only flew to the other ear and went buzz-z-z until the goat thought there must

be some dreadful thing in the turnip field. So out through the hole in the fence he went, and down the road he ran to the pasture.

The bumblebee flew to the second goat and buzz-z-z she went first in one ear and then in the other, until that goat wanted nothing else but to run through the hole in the fence and down the road to the pasture.

The bumblebee flew after the third goat and buzzed first in one ear and then in the other until he, too, was glad to follow the other goats through the hole in the fence and down the road to the pasture.

"Thank you, little bee," said Johnny, and wiping away his tears, he hurried down the road to drive the goats into the pasture.

Wading

Now come, the water isn't cold,
Give us your hands and we'll take hold;
It's splendid when you once are in,
And quite, quite safe, so just begin!

Look how the little ripple goes
All curling softly round your toes!
And look, you won't be blamed, my pet,
However dripping wet you get!

ANNE ANDERSON

ANNE.....
ANDERSON

The Dumb Soldier

When the grass was closely mown,
Walking on the lawn alone,
In the turf a hole I found
And hid a soldier underground.

Spring and daisies came apace;
Grasses hide my hiding place;
Grasses run like a green sea
O'er the lawn up to my knee.

Under grass alone he lies,
Looking up with leaden eyes,
Scarlet coat and pointed gun,
To the stars and to the sun.

When the grass is ripe like grain,
When the scythe is stoned again,
When the lawn is shaven clear,
Then my hole shall reappear.

I shall find him, never fear,
I shall find my grenadier;

But for all that's gone and come,
I shall find my soldier dumb.

He has lived, a little thing,
In the grassy woods of spring;
Done, if he could tell me true,
Just as I should like to do.

He has seen the starry hours
And the springing of the flowers;
And the fairy things that pass
In the forests of the grass.

In the silence he has heard
Talking bee and ladybird,
And the butterfly has flown,
O'er him as he lay alone.

Not a word will he disclose,
Not a word of all he knows.
I must lay him on the shelf,
And make up the tale myself.

ROBERT LOUIS STEVENSON

The Travels of a Fox

A fox was digging behind a tree stump one day and found a bumblebee. He put the bumblebee into a bag and went on his way.

He went into the first house he came to: "May I leave my bag here while I go to Squintum's?" the fox asked the mistress of the house.

"Certainly," said the woman.

"You must be careful not to open the bag," said the fox.

As soon as the fox was out of sight, the woman opened the bag to take a little peep inside. Out flew the bumblebee, and the woman's rooster caught him and ate him up.

After a while the fox came back. He picked up his bag, looked inside, and discovered that his bumblebee was gone.

"Where is my bumblebee?" he asked the woman.

"I just untied the bag, and the bumblebee flew out, and the rooster ate him up," she replied.

"I must have the rooster then," said the fox.

So he caught the rooster, put him into his bag, and traveled on.

At the next house he came to, he asked the mistress of the house: "May I leave my bag here while I go to Squintum's?"

"Of course," said the woman.

"You must be careful not to open the bag," said the fox.

But as soon as the fox was out of sight, the woman took just a little peep into the bag. The rooster flew out, and the woman's pig caught him and ate him up.

After a while the fox came back. He picked up his bag and he realized that the rooster was not in it.

"Where is my rooster?" he asked the woman.

And the woman said, "I just untied the bag, and the rooster flew out, and the pig ate him."

"I must have the pig then," said the fox.

So he caught the pig, put him into his bag, and traveled on.

The fox went into the next house he came to and asked the mistress of the house: "May I leave my bag here while I go to Squintum's?"

"Yes," said the woman.

"You must be careful not to open the bag," said the fox.

But as soon as the fox was out of sight, the woman untied the bag just to take a little peep inside. The pig jumped out and the woman's ox ate him.

After a while the fox came back. He picked up his bag and realized that the pig was gone. "Where is my pig?" he asked the woman.

"I just untied the bag, and the pig jumped out, and the ox ate him," replied the woman.

"I must have the ox then," said the fox.

So he caught the ox, put him into his bag, and traveled on.

He went into the next house he came to and asked the mistress of the house, "May I leave my bag here while I go to Squintum's?"

"Yes, you may," replied the woman.

"Be careful not to open the bag," said the fox.

But as soon as the fox was out of sight, the woman took just a little peep into

the bag. The ox got out and the woman's little boy chased him far away over the fields.

After a while the fox came back. He picked up his bag and realized that his ox was gone.

"Where is my ox?" he asked the woman.

"I just untied the string, the ox got out, and my little boy chased him far away over the fields."

"I must have the little boy then," said the fox.

So he caught the little boy, put him into his bag, and traveled on.

When he came to the next house, he went in and asked the mistress of the house: "May I leave my bag here while I go to Squintum's?"

"Yes," said the woman.

"Be careful not to open the bag," said the fox as he left.

The woman had just made a cake, and her children were around her asking for some.

"Oh, Mother, give me a piece of cake," said one child. "Please, Mother, give me a piece," said the others.

The delicious smell of the cake reached the little boy who was crying in the bag. He heard the children asking for cake and he said, "Oh, please, give me a piece of cake, too."

The woman opened the bag and took the little boy out. Then she put her watchdog into the bag in the little boy's place.

The little boy stopped crying and he and the other children ate the delicious cake.

After a while the fox came back. He picked up his bag and he saw that it was tightly tied, so he put it over his back and traveled far into the woods. Then he sat down and untied the bag.

If the little boy had been in the bag, things might have gone badly for him. But the little boy was safe at the woman's house, and when the fox untied the bag the watchdog jumped out. When the fox saw the angry watchdog he ran into the woods. He ran and he ran and he was never seen again.

The Cow

The friendly cow all red and white,
  I love with all my heart:
She gives me cream with all her might,
  To eat with apple tart.

She wanders lowing here and there,
  And yet she cannot stray,
All in the pleasant open air,
  The pleasant light of day;

And blown by all the winds that pass
  And wet with all the showers,
She walks among the meadow grass
  And eats the meadow flowers.

ROBERT LOUIS STEVENSON

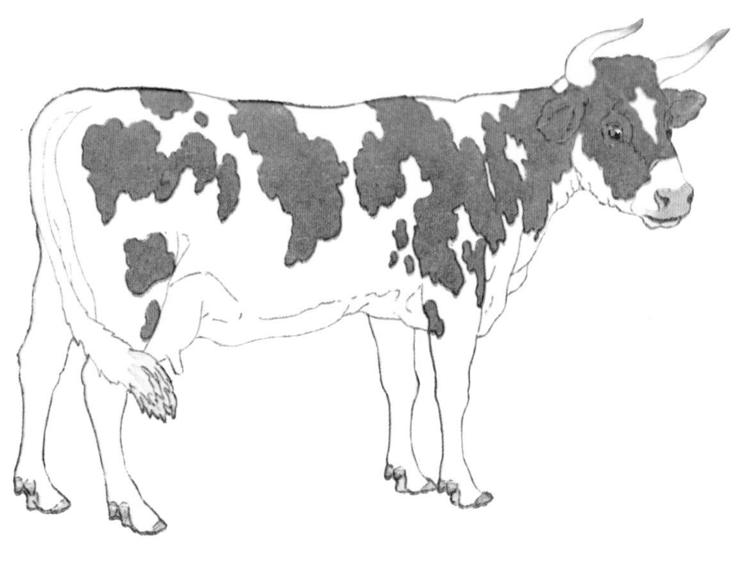

A Fairy Went a-Marketing

A fairy went a-marketing—
  She bought a little fish;
She put it in a crystal bowl
  Upon a golden dish.
An hour she sat in wonderment
  And watched its silver gleam,
And then she gently took it up
  And slipped it in a stream.

A fairy went a-marketing—
  She bought a colored bird;
It sang the sweetest, shrillest song
  That ever she had heard.
She sat beside its painted cage
  And listened half the day,
And then she opened wide the door
  And let it fly away.

A fairy went a-marketing—
  She bought a winter gown
All stitched about with gossamer
  And lined with thistledown.
She wore it all the afternoon
  With prancing and delight,
Then gave it to a little frog
  To keep him warm at night.

A fairy went a-marketing—
  She bought a gentle mouse
To take her tiny messages,
  To keep her tiny house.
All day she kept its busy feet
  Pit-patting to and fro,
And then she kissed its silken ears,
  Thanked it, and let it go.

ROSE FYLEMAN

Summer Night

The summer nights we dearly love,
With scents below and stars above—
When all the skies are darkly blue,
And all the grass is deep in dew.

But if the stars were dim, no doubt
We still could find our way about.
For just see here! this glowworm bright
Would be our lantern all the night!

Anne Anderson

The Bremen Town Musicians

There was once a donkey who was old and tired. For many, many years he had worked hard carrying heavy sacks of flour for his master, the miller. But he was no longer strong and he could not carry the heavy sacks of flour anymore.

One cold evening, when the donkey was waiting for his food, he heard the miller say to his wife, "We cannot afford to feed the old donkey much longer. He worked hard for us for many years, but now he can hardly carry even one sack of flour. He's not earning his keep. Perhaps we should sell him to the glue factory."

The poor old donkey was very frightened. He knew he must leave the mill. No matter what happened to him, it would be better than being made into glue.

After everyone had gone to sleep, the donkey quietly left his stall and began walking down the road that led to the town of Bremen.

When he had gone a little way, the donkey saw an old hound dog lying at the side of the road.

"Hello!" said the donkey. "Why are you lying at the side of the road?"

"Oh," said the dog, "just because I am old and tired. I seem to get weaker every day, and I can no longer go hunting with my master. I worked hard for him for many years since I was a puppy, but a few days ago I heard him say I was good for nothing but cat meat. So I have left him, but how shall I earn my living now?"

"I just got a good idea," said the donkey. "I can still bray quite well and I'm sure you can howl. Let's go to Bremen. We can join the town band. I'm sure they will be delighted to have us."

The dog liked the idea, and they went on together. They had walked only a few miles when they saw an old gray cat. She was sitting on a wall near the road. Her face was as sad as three rainy days.

"Good morning," the donkey said to the cat. "You certainly are not looking very happy this sunny morning."

"How can I be happy when I'm in danger of being drowned," answered the cat.

"Why are you in danger of being drowned?" asked the hound dog.

"Because I am advanced in years," replied the cat, "and my teeth are blunt, and I like sitting close to the fire and purring better than I like chasing mice. My mistress always liked to play with me. She even liked me to sleep on her bed. But now that I can't catch mice she wants to drown me. I have managed to escape. But where shall I go?"

"Come with us to Bremen," said the donkey. "We are going to join the town band. I'm sure you can howl quite well. You can become a town musician, too." The cat thought it was a wonderful idea and decided to go with them.

The three companions trudged along until they came to a farmyard. There on the gate sat an old rooster looking as sad as sad could be.

"What is the matter with you?" asked the donkey.

"I always protected the hens and chicks in the farmyard," said the rooster, "and I always woke my master and mistress in the morning. But now I'm old and because I sometimes sleep a little late in the morning, the mistress has no pity on me. She has told the cook to put me into the soup tomorrow. They will wring my neck in the morning and eat me for their Sunday supper."

"Well," said the donkey, "you had better come with us. We are going to Bremen to join the town band. I'm sure you can still cock-a-doodle when you want to."

"Of course I can," said the rooster, who stood up straight, flapped his wings, and crowed "Cock-a-doodle-doo!" as well as any young rooster.

"That was wonderful," said the cat. "You have a good voice. You must go to Bremen with us."

The rooster liked the idea very much, so off went the four together. But they could not reach the town of Bremen in the remaining hours of daylight. And they were getting tired and hungry. To make it worse, it got very cold as the sun went down.

Finally, they came to some woods, where they agreed to spend the night. The donkey and the dog and the cat laid themselves down under a large fir tree. The rooster flew up to the very top, where he would feel safest. Before he went to sleep he looked all around. He thought he saw a light twinkling in the distance.

"I think I see a light," he called to his companions. "There must be a house not far off."

The donkey said, "Then we must rise and go to it, for the lodgings here are very bad."

The hound dog said, "Yes, and few bones with a little meat on them would do me good."

"I would like to curl up near a blazing fire. It's very cold here," said the cat.

The rooster led them through the dark woods. Soon they came to a fine stone house near a brook. There was a bright light shining in one of the downstairs windows. The four friends huddled together and whispered as they tried to decide what to do next. Finally, it was agreed that the cat should leap up on a windowsill and look into the room.

"What did you see?" asked the rooster when she returned.

"I saw a table laden with wonderful food," replied the old cat. "There's a blazing fire and on the floor there are piles of gold and silver and jewels. The men who are eating and drinking must be robbers."

"This house would do nicely for us," said the rooster.

"So would the food," said the donkey, who was very hungry.

"So would something to drink," said the hound dog, who was very thirsty.

"Yes, indeed, if we were only inside the house instead of those robbers," replied the donkey.

"Perhaps we should make some music for them," said the donkey. "Then they might give us something to eat and drink." As quietly as they could, the four friends went to the window.

The donkey placed his forefeet on the windowsill. The hound dog climbed on the donkey's back. The cat leaped onto the dog's back. The rooster then flew up and perched himself on the cat's head.

Then, at a signal, they began their music all together. The donkey brayed, the hound dog and the cat howled, and the rooster crowed.

At the dreadful noise, the robbers screamed and jumped from their seats. In great fright, convinced that nothing less than demons were outside their house, they ran into the woods as fast as they could.

The four friends were delighted, although their plan had not worked quite as they expected. They went into the house, sat down at the table, and had a huge feast. They then said good-night to each other, put out the light, and each one looked for a suitable and comfortable place to sleep.

The donkey found some bundles of straw in the shed and made a cozy bed. The hound dog lay down behind the door. The cat curled up on the hearth near the warm ashes. The rooster set himself on the hen roost, where he roosted quite comfortably. They were all tired from their long journey, and now that they were warm and full of good food and drink they quickly went to sleep.

Shortly after midnight, the robbers looked out from their hiding place in the woods. They could see that no lights were burning in the house and it was very quiet. The captain said, "We should not have let ourselves be frightened so easily." He sent one of the robbers back to examine the house to see what he could find.

Still very fearful, the robber crawled through an open window. Everything was quiet, so he went into the kitchen to light a candle. All was dark except for the cat's shining fiery eyes. The robber thought they were live coals and stooped down and poked his candle in the cat's eye. The cat was furious and leaped at his face, spat at him, and scratched him.

The robber, who was dreadfully frightened, was running out the back door when the dog, who was lying there, jumped up and bit his leg.

.As he ran through the yard, past the shed, the donkey gave him a good kick with his hind foot.

The rooster, who had been awakened by the noise, called out, "Cock-a-doodle-doo!"

The robber ran as fast as he could back to the captain. "In the house there is a horrid old witch," he cried. "She flew at me, and scratched my face with her long fingernails. And near the door there is a man with a knife, who stabbed me in the leg. In the shed there is a black monster, who hit me with a club. And up on the roof there sits a judge, who called out, 'Catch the thief! Oh, do!' So I ran away as fast as I could."

The robbers were so frightened that they never returned to the house. But the four musicians liked it so well that they decided not to continue their journey to Bremen. So the four friends spent the rest of their days in comfort. And every evening they practiced their singing and made lovely music together.

The Land of Nod

From breakfast on all through the day
At home among my friends I stay;
But every night I go abroad
Afar into the land of Nod.

All by myself I have to go,
With none to tell me what to do—
All alone beside the streams
And up the mountainsides of dreams.

The strangest things are there for me,
Both things to eat and things to see,
And many frightening sights abroad
Till morning in the land of Nod.

Try as I like to find the way,
I never can get back by day,
Nor can remember plain and clear
The curious music that I hear.

ROBERT LOUIS STEVENSON

The Silver Road

Last night I saw a silver road
  Go straight across the sea;
And quick as I raced along the shore,
  That quick road followed me.

It followed me all round the bay,
  Where small waves danced in tune;
And at the end of the silver road
  There hung a silver moon.

A large round moon on a pale green sky,
  With a pathway bright and broad,
Some night I shall bring that silver moon
  Across that silver road!

HAMISH HENDRY

The Little Elf

I met a little Elf-man, once,
Down where the lilies blow.
I asked him why he was so small,
And why he didn't grow.

He slightly frowned, and with his eye
He looked me through and through.
"I'm quite as big for me," said he,
"As you are big for you."

JOHN KENDRICK BANGS

The Little Land

When at home alone I sit
And am very tired of it,
I have just to shut my eyes
To go sailing through the skies—
To go sailing far away
To the pleasant Land of Play;
To the fairyland and afar
Where the Little People are;
Where the clover tops are trees,
And the rain pools are the seas,
And the leaves, like little ships,
Sail about on tiny trips;

And above the daisy tree
   Through the grasses,
High o'erhead the bumblebee
   Hums and passes.

In that forest to and fro
I can wander, I can go;
See the spider and the fly,
And the ants go marching by
Carrying parcels with their feet
Down the green and grassy street.

I can in the sorrel sit
Where the ladybird alit.
I can climb the jointed grass
   And on high
See the greater swallows pass
   In the sky,
And the round sun rolling by
Heeding no such things as I.

Through that forest I can pass
Till, as in a looking-glass,
Humming fly and daisy tree
And my tiny self I see
Painted very clear and neat
On the rain pool at my feet.
Should a leaflet come to land
Drifting near to where I stand,
Straight I'll board that tiny boat
Round the rain pool sea to float.

Little thoughtful creatures sit
On the grassy coasts of it;
Little things with lovely eyes
See me sailing with surprise.
Some are clad in armor green—
(These have sure to battle been!)
Some are pied with ev'ry hue,
Black and crimson, gold and blue;
Some have wings and swift are gone;
But they all look kindly on.

When my eyes I once again
Open, and see all things plain:
High bare walls, great bare floor;
Great big knobs on drawer and door;
Great big people perched on chairs,
Stitching tucks and mending tears,
Each a hill that I could climb,
And talking nonsense all the time—
O dear me,
That I could be
A sailor on the rain pool sea,
A climber in the clover tree,
And just come back, a sleepyhead,
Late at night to go to bed.

ROBERT LOUIS STEVENSON